About the Book

Jamestown, founded in 1607, was the first English colony to survive in the American wilderness. Settlers who went to Jamestown faced many trials—owing to lack of practical skills, to disease, to starvation, and to periodic Indian attacks. But colonists continued to cross the Atlantic, and in the process a new spirit was starting to form: "These men who had gone to Virginia were becoming fiercely independent, so that no power could control them; Virginians would dare anything where their rights were at stake."

For ninety-two years Jamestown was the capital of Virginia and the locale of many events which would set precedents for the development of the South and of the nation as a whole. Burke Davis provides the young reader with an absorbing chronicle of Jamestown's history and its way of life in these early years.

About the Author

Burke Davis is the author of more than twenty books for both adults and young readers, including novels, biographies, and histories. He lives in Williamsburg, Virginia, where he is on the staff of the restoration. He has worked in the field of Colonial Virginia history for a number of years and has written about it in several books.

Mr. Davis is a native of North Carolina, where he attended Duke University, Guilford College, and the University of North Carolina. He spent twenty years as a newspaperman in North Carolina and in Baltimore, Maryland. His wife, the former Evangeline McLennan, is general manager and editor of the *Virginia Gazette*, the nation's oldest newspaper.

About the Illustrator

Tran Mawicke is a free-lance illustrator of books and magazines. He was born in Chicago and studied at the Art Institute of Chicago. He is a past president of the Society of Illustrators and an official artist for the U.S. Air Force. Mr. Mawicke and his wife have four children; they live in Bronxville, New York.

About the Getting to Know *Books*

The *Getting to Know* books offer a wide range of exciting and valuable information about countries throughout the world, including the efforts of worldwide organizations. These round-the-world books are designed to give an up-to-date portrait of a land and its people. Concentrating on the everyday life and customs of a region, they incorporate its geography and history, as well as highlight *what's new today.* To keep pace with the fast-changing times, each book is revised periodically.

In addition to this group of international titles, the *Getting to Know* books now include a number of detailed accounts of states and regions within our own country. Everyday life is viewed with a keen historical eye, aimed to give the reader a clear picture of the role each area has played in the development of the nation as a whole. Each book devotes particular attention to the study of historical landmarks which can still be seen today.

Getting to know

JAMESTOWN

by

BURKE DAVIS

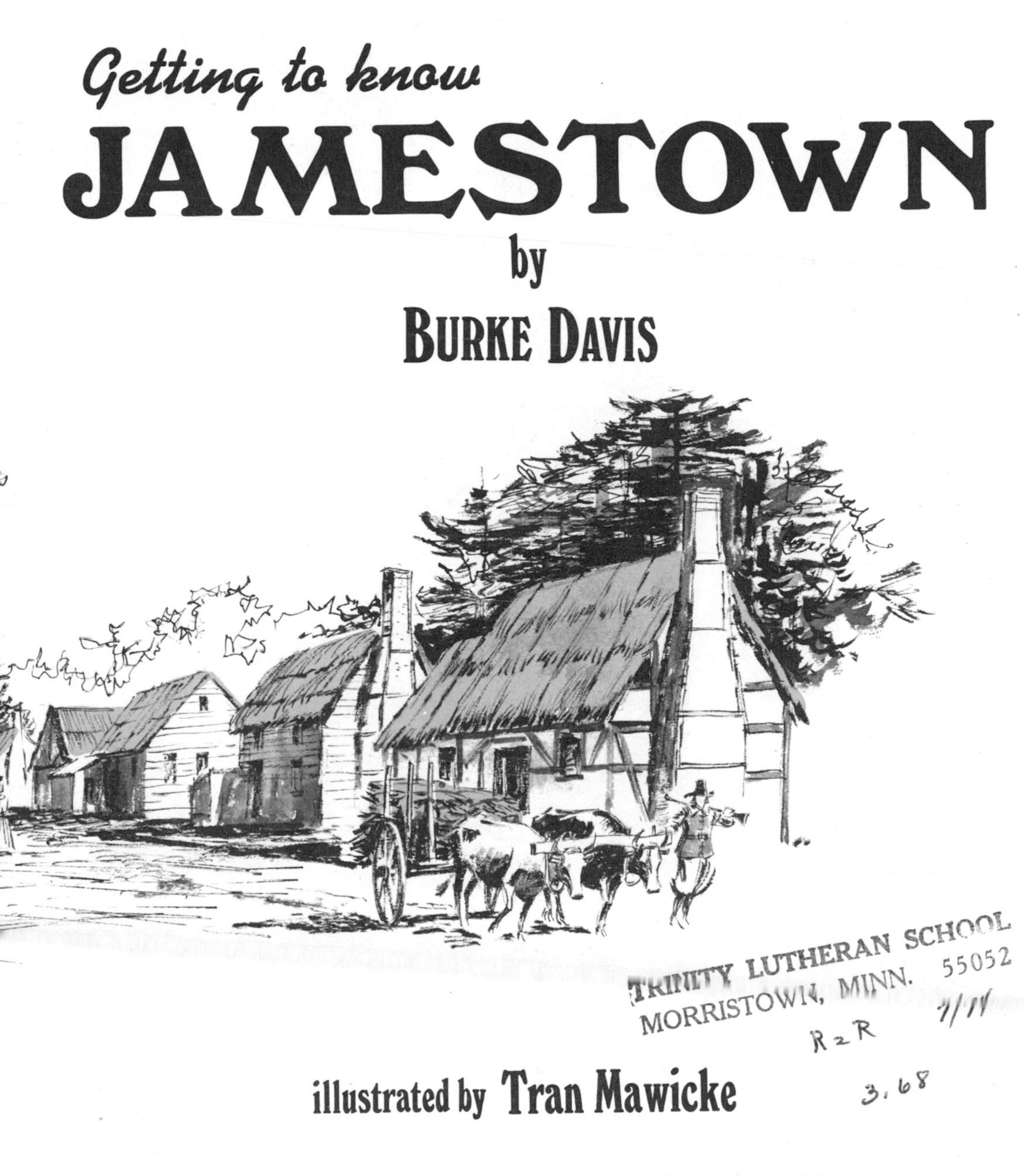

illustrated by **Tran Mawicke**

Coward, McCann & Geoghegan, Inc. New York

Published simultaneously in Canada by Longmans Canada Limited, Toronto.

Library of Congress Catalog Card Number: 73-132601
PRINTED IN THE UNITED STATES OF AMERICA
08212

SBN: GB 698-30130-7

Second Impression

At four o'clock on Sunday morning, April 26, in the year 1607, three storm-beaten little English ships sailed within sight of the Virginia shore. They were four months out of London, their men worn by the struggle against the wild Atlantic, tired of being packed like sardines into tiny holds, of drinking foul water from slimy casks, hungry for good English food. As they drew nearer the coast in the light of the rising sun, the 144 men aboard the vessels rejoiced.

The *Susan Constant*, the *Godspeed*, and the much smaller *Discovery* anchored in Chesapeake Bay and the men hurried ashore. The first successful English colony in America had been planted. One of the great migrations of history had begun.

The dunes were overgrown with holly and thickets of sweet-smelling bayberry, and with dwarfed evergreen oaks that had been shaped by sea winds. Beyond, the Englishmen saw great forests of pine and cypress and hardwood trees, where dogwood and redbud were in bloom. Wild strawberries grew like carpets on the ground. The men had glimpses of strange birds and animals. One of the party, George Percy, wrote of the beautiful country: "fair meadows and goodly tall trees, with such fresh waters running through the woods as I was almost ravished at the first sight."

The men built a crude wooden cross on the sands and their chaplain, The Reverend Robert Hunt, led them in a prayer of thanksgiving for their safe arrival in the new land. But dim forms stirred in the shadows of the underbrush, and the settlers were suddenly attacked. Naked brown men with painted bodies scrambled down the dunes on all fours with bows in their mouths and then ran toward the Englishmen, shooting arrows and yelling. Two settlers fell wounded. Someone fired a musket, and the frightened Indians disappeared in the thickets. Red men and Englishmen had begun a long war for the North American continent that was to last nearly three hundred years.

That night, by campfires on the beach, the settlers opened orders brought from home, instructions from King James' Council. Captain Christopher Newport, who had commanded during the voyage, found some surprises in the sealed box. He must now take orders from a council of the settlers—and one of them was the most quarrelsome man in the party. Captain John Smith had been kept in chains on the voyage, under arrest for mutiny. But Smith was a veteran soldier, the one man of the colony who knew how to meet the dangers of a strange and hostile country. The orders also told the settlers to sail up a river leading westward, where they would be safe from raiding ships of Spain, with which England was at war. To protect itself from enemies the colony was to build a fort on an island.

Early the next morning the ships moved inland up a broad river and sailed for several days between its wooded shores, looking for a place to land. At last, about the middle of May, they went ashore on a tree-grown point that thrust far into the river.

The water was so deep that they sailed the ships to shore and tied their hemp cables to the great trees. The point was almost an island, joined to the mainland by a narrow neck of land, a low, marshy place where clouds of insects hung in the warm air. Still, it would be easy to protect. It was less than three miles long, and its width varied from three hundred yards to a mile and a quarter.

They named the spot Jamestown and the river the James, in honor of their king. When they had moved ashore with supplies, tools, arms, and clothing, the settlers divided into three groups for their first work in the new world: Some were to build a fort and storehouse, others to dig and plant gardens, and a third group to explore the nearby country. Axes began to ring in the virgin forest, smoke rose, English cocks crowed, and English hogs rooted in the deep rich soil. And natives who watched from hiding heard the strange sounds of English voices.

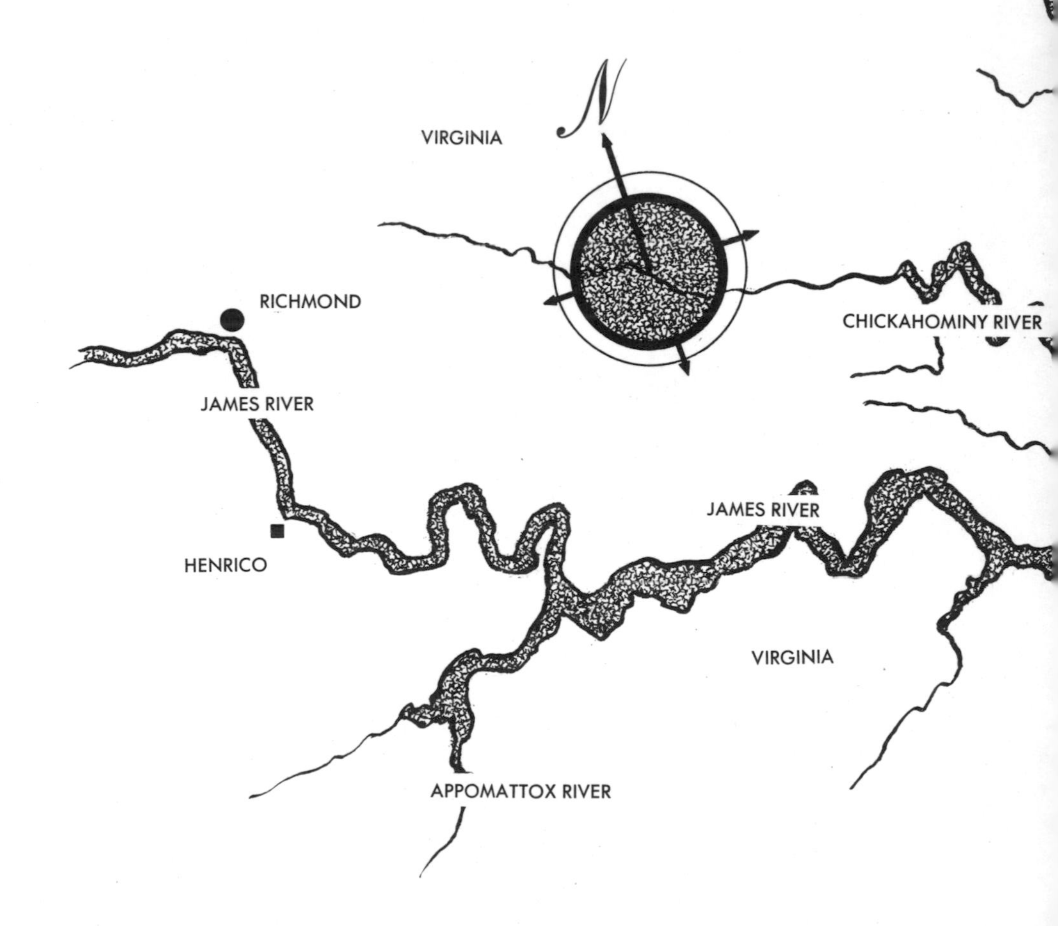

These men, however, were poorly prepared to conquer the wilderness. Most of them came from English cities and would not live through the hardships to be met in the unspoiled lands which lay before them, lands which would not be fully settled until the time of their great-great-great grandchildren. There were some skilled men in the colony—a surgeon, a tailor, a mason, a blacksmith, a barber, several carpenters and bricklayers, some soldiers, and a sailor. But about half of them were "gentlemen," who had come as leaders and planners, and would be of little help in the grim struggle against nature and hostile Indians. The colony

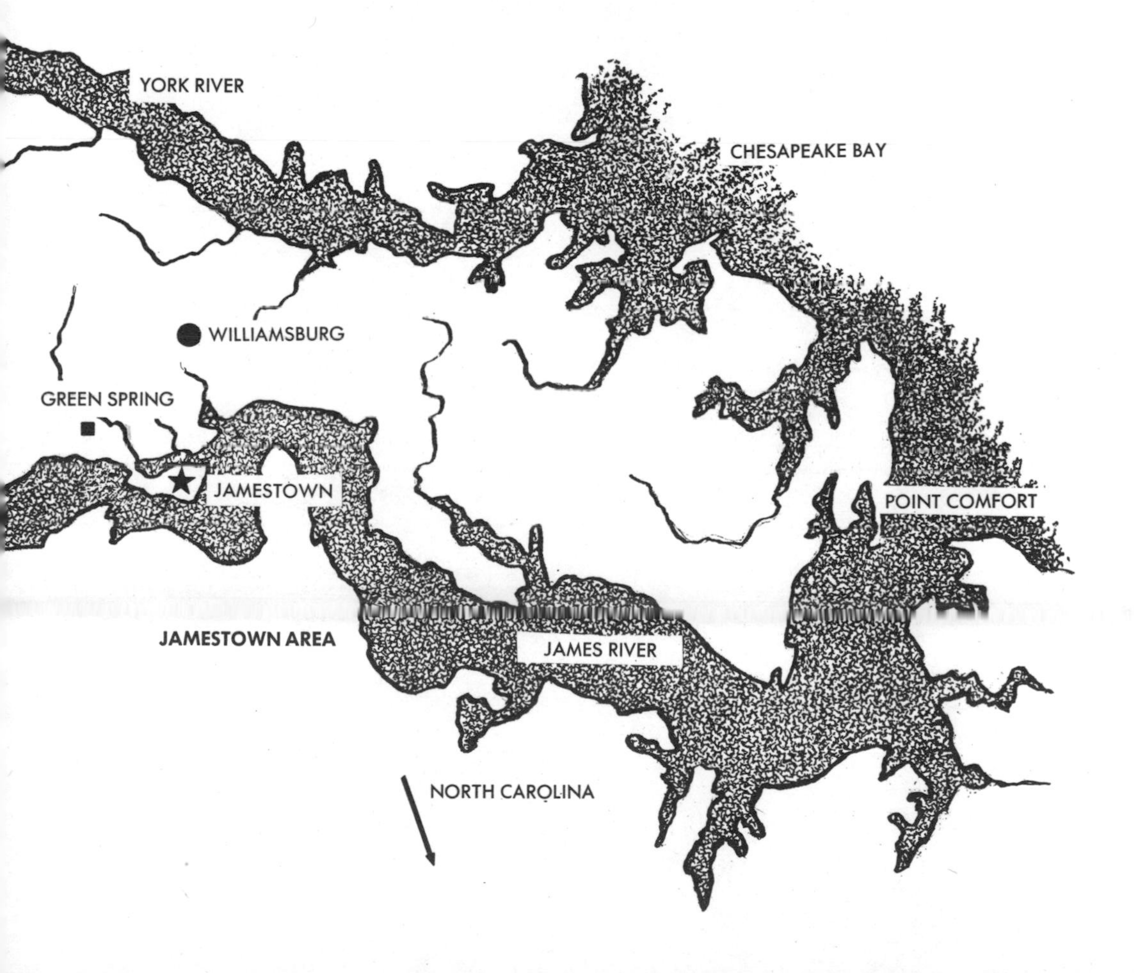

was armed with three small cannon, which were mounted in the triangular fort, with muskets which seldom hit their targets, with swords, iron helmets and breastplates, and a few sharp weapons mounted on poles, called halberds.

SIR WALTER RALEIGH

They were not the first Europeans to come into this land. More than forty years earlier Spanish priests had sailed into the Chesapeake, which they called the Bay of the Mother of God, had passed by the site of Jamestown and moved up the marshy creeks to camp on higher ground. This colony was wiped out when Indians massacred the priests, all but one, who escaped and somehow made his way back to a Spanish ship. Englishmen had also come earlier. Not far to the south, a sail of two or three days, the adventurous Sir Walter Raleigh had planted a colony on the shore of what was to become North Carolina. That colony had also vanished, with men, women, and children, leaving behind only a mysterious message carved on a tree: the single Indian word, *Croatan.*

A few days after the men of Jamestown went ashore, Captain Newport, John Smith, and others explored up the James, and while they were gone a large band of Indians attacked the fort, killing a man and a boy and wounding a dozen others. For weeks afterward Indians lay in the marsh grass and reeds outside the fort, shooting settlers who strayed beyond the palisade.

The two larger ships returned to England in June, leaving the colony to a time of terrible suffering. Soon the only food left was wormy barley and wheat and a few crabs and fish, and the only drink was brackish water from the river. The summer heat brought disease, Indians continued to attack, and by September almost half of the colony had died, many of them from hunger. George Percy wrote of the "pitiful murmurings and outcries of our sick men without relief, every day and night, for six weeks."

The colony was saved by the Indians of Chief Powhatan's tribe, who suddenly became friendly and brought meat, bread, fish, and corn. Thousands of waterfowl landed on the rivers in their fall migration, and Jamestown hunters killed many of them. With new strength, the men went to work under the direction of John Smith, who was finally named president of the council after others had failed.

CAPTAIN JOHN SMITH

The men soon learned that Smith was a true leader. He was only twenty-seven years old, the son of a tenant farmer, but already he was a man of many adventures. Since the age of sixteen he had roamed the world as a soldier, serving in several armies. He was only five feet tall, with a red beard and a boastful manner. He was energetic, forceful, and intelligent, and quickly taught his men to cut the reeds and grass near the fort, to thatch the houses they built, and to make nets for fishing. He had a well dug inside the fort, one of "excellent sweete water," and built a log blockhouse on the neck of land leading to the mainland, to halt the coming and going of Indians. He had many chickens and hogs raised, built two small forts on the opposite side of the river, explored the countryside, and traded with the Indians. Always, Captain Smith worked harder than any of his men.

Supply ships came from England during the first winter, with five hundred more men and the first two women, one of them Ann Burras, a maidservant who married John Laydon in the first recorded English marriage in America. In the same ships were eight Dutchmen and Poles, men who made glass, soap, tar, and pitch for the colony and began the first tiny American industries.

The new ships also brought more trouble, for the sailors found some glittering stones that they thought were gold. Gold fever swept the colony as men loaded a ship with the worthless stone, pyrite, known as fool's gold. One settler wrote in disgust of how the sailors "made all men their slaves. . . . There was no talk, no hope, no work, but dig gold, wash gold, refine gold, load gold." The new ships sailed for home in April, 1608, when the colony was almost a year old.

Captain Smith was captured by Indians a few months later. He had killed two warriors before he was overcome, and Powhatan sentenced him to death. Smith was led before the chief for execution and forced to kneel with his head on a stone so that Indians with clubs could beat out his brains—but Powhatan's daughter, Pocahontas, rushed to the captain, took his head in her lap, and begged her father to spare Smith's life. There were those who did not believe this story Smith told of his rescue, but he had escaped captivity, Powhatan's tribes did become friendly, and young Pocahontas afterward played in the streets of Jamestown.

When Smith returned to Jamestown, he found that rats had ruined the supply of grain and that men and animals faced starvation. He halted work at the fort and divided the colony so that it could survive—some went down the river to gather oysters, others to Point Comfort on the Chesapeake to live in a fishing camp, others up the river, and a few to live in Indian villages. The worst was over when spring came, and Smith had lost only seven or eight men from starvation.

While the colony was struggling for its life, men in London were making plans to strengthen the settlement so that it might overcome its troubles and last forever. A new company was formed, called the Virginia Company, one of the world's first private corporations. Its money was furnished by groups of London craftsmen and merchants, businessmen and noblemen, men who hoped to make a profit from the expedition, many of whom were to sail to Virginia themselves. Despite the earlier disappointment, these Englishmen still thought the country was rich in gold and silver and that huge nuggets lay on the ground. They also thought the new land was on the route to Asia, where even richer treasures were waiting. They were eager for personal wealth, but the colony was also meant to expand English power and trade. English businessmen hoped to find markets in the new world and within a few years were importing valuable goods—especially tobacco and timber. In return they shipped more English goods to Virginia each year.

In the summer of 1609 a new governor arrived with nine ships and about three hundred men, women, and children. This first governor was Sir Thomas West, Lord De La Warr (Delaware), a well-educated man who had been prominent in the English court. The Virginia Company had appointed him governor of Virginia for life. Once more this new group of colonists made life harder for those already in Jamestown. Those who arrived were weak and ill and increased Captain John Smith's burdens. The captain was badly burned in an explosion of gunpowder, and near the end of 1609, he returned to England. His place was taken by George Percy, who was not so strong a leader as John Smith.

The captain thought he had left the colony well prepared for troubles that were still to come, with three ships and seven boats, provisions for ten weeks, plenty of stores to trade to Indians, twenty-four cannon, three hundred muskets, five hundred swords, tools, fishing nets, seven horses, five hundred to six hundred hogs, five hundred chickens, and a few sheep and goats. But Smith had hardly left Virginia when Indians attacked once more. The tribesmen were enraged because the white men had invaded their country, driving them from fishing and hunting grounds used by their people for hundreds of years. When settlers built houses and forts, wild game was driven away and food became scarce. The arrival of the colonists seemed a threat to the Indians' entire way of life.

Smith's outposts were destroyed. When Percy sent men to Powhatan for food, thirty-four of them were killed and their leader, Captain John Ratcliffe, was tortured to death—Indian women scraped the flesh from his body with shells. Other Indians circled the Jamestown fort and cut off all supplies. Food gave out quickly, and the settlers ate horses, dogs, cats, rats, and snakes, and even the dead from their graves. Men and women who were starving crept into the woods in their last hours, dug holes, covered themselves with leaves, and died. By spring only sixty of the four hundred and ninety settlers left by Smith were still alive, and when a relief ship came in May, the discouraged colonists were ready to give up. They boarded the ship and sailed down the James on the way to England, but near the mouth of the river they met a new party of three hundred men under Lord De La Warr, who persuaded the colonists to return to their small town. Fresh supplies were brought in. The decaying fort was rebuilt, the church restored, and a new government set up. Lord De La Warr then returned to England for help. The settlement was saved once more. The "starving time" was over.

By 1611, Sir Thomas Dale arrived with three hundred more people and livestock and supplies. Dale, an old soldier, replaced George Percy as leader of the colony. He arrived to find most of the colonists "at their daily and usual work, bowling in the streets," and put them to work. Soon afterward six more ships arrived, bringing more craftsmen and women and children and many cattle. The colonists built a new city inland near the site of present Richmond, a town they called Henrico.

Dale also made war on the Indians and did not try to make friends as Captain Smith had done. When Powhatan's tribe attacked an outpost and refused to give up captives taken there, Dale burned some Indian villages and killed many of their people, including a chief's wife and children. Some tribes were driven from the neighborhood, and only friendly ones remained. There was peace near Jamestown for many years.

The chief reason for the peace between Indians and whites was Powhatan's daughter Pocahontas, who had grown up to become a beautiful young woman of eighteen. In 1613, while she was visiting in a village on the Potomac River, Pocahontas was betrayed by a cousin and sold to an English captain, Samuel Argall, for the price of a copper kettle. Argall took her aboard his ship and carried her to the new town of Henrico, to be held as a hostage. Sir Thomas Dale ordered that the girl be taught English and instructed in the Christian religion, and she was soon baptized and given the Christian name of Rebecca. In Henrico, Pocahontas met and fell in love with John Rolfe, a planter who had recently come to Virginia and who had lost his wife in a shipwreck. The two were married in April, 1614.

Rolfe had already become one of Virginia's most important men, as founder of the American tobacco trade which was to bring vast wealth to this and other Southern colonies. In 1611 or 1612 Rolfe had bought tobacco seed from a sea captain who had come up from the West Indies, and in the late summer of 1612 the rich soil produced a crop of tobacco with broad golden leaves, the first of the Virginia type which was to become famous. The new leaf caused a sensation in London, where smokers quickly made it popular. Within five years Virginia was shipping more than forty-thousand pounds a year to England. Rolfe and other planters began to grow rich.

Some colonists moved to nearby plantations to grow tobacco, and others left the fort to settle outside. Jamestown became a village of small houses, huddled against one another along wandering cart tracks which served as streets. New settlements were founded, all of them busy raising tobacco from John Rolfe's seed.

In 1616 Rolfe and his wife Pocahontas and their young son Thomas sailed to England. With them were a dozen or more other Indians on their way to be educated there. The Rolfes spent a year in England and were entertained by the queen, the Bishop of London, and other British leaders. When Pocahontas appeared at court, one observer said, she "carried herself as the daughter of a King." The Indian princess was never to see Virginia again. She died of a white man's disease in England as she was about to sail for home. John Rolfe returned alone, leaving his son Thomas to be given an English education and to sail back to Virginia many years later. Thousands of descendants of Pocahontas and John Rolfe live in America today.

John Rolfe returned to Virginia and found the colonists had gone mad over tobacco. The leaf was now used as money, and Jamestown was almost deserted, with its streets planted in tobacco. King James, who said that smoking was harmful to the brain and lungs, tried to stop Englishmen who spent "most of their time in that idle vanity." But the tobacco trade continued to grow in spite of the king's disapproval, new taxes, and occasional poor crops. Because many Virginians raised only tobacco and often had little to eat, Governor Dale ordered Jamestown's growers to raise two acres of corn for every man at work in the fields.

Rolfe found other troubles at Jamestown. Virginia deer, on which the colony depended, had almost disappeared when an unknown disease swept through the herds. A great hail storm damaged corn and tobacco crops, and Governor De La Warr died on a sea voyage. But even now more improvements were being made in London.

A new governor, Captain George Yeardley, arrived at Jamestown early in 1619 and opened one of the most important years in the life of the colony. Eleven ships came during that year, bringing more than twelve hundred settlers, ninety of them women. These "young, handsome and honestly educated maids" had been sent to marry the colonists. The Virginia Company ordered the governor and council to care for these young women until they "happened upon good matches. . . . not enforcing them to marry against their wills." Some of the girls married very quickly, but others flirted with the men of Jamestown. A few of the girls even became engaged to several men at the same time! The assembly soon passed a law forbidding this. Husbands paid one hundred and twenty pounds of tobacco for the Atlantic passage of these brides, and the couples settled down to make new lives in the wilderness.

In the same year one hundred boys and girls arrived from London to become apprentices and learn trades. Many others who could not afford their passage by ship from England came as indentured servants. To repay their fare across the Atlantic, they were bound to serve their masters (usually for seven years) before being freed to live on their own. These servants were forced to obey their masters throughout the term of their contract, and the masters were bound to feed and clothe them and teach them trades from which they could earn their living. The men who arrived in this year were not like some who had come earlier, but were "choice men, born and bred up to labor and industry." About two hundred and fifty of them came from the English counties of Devon, Warwickshire, Staffordshire, and Sussex and were trained in skilled trades. It was a welcome change from the shiploads of poor and unskilled people who had been gathered from London's streets in other years and shipped to Virginia to rid England of its unemployed.

Another important event of 1619 was the arrival of the first black men in America. A Dutch ship had been raiding Spanish colonies in the West Indies and had taken about twenty Negroes as prisoners. This ship reached Jamestown in late August, 1619. Supplies had run low, and the captain traded these unfortunate people for food. Some of the Negroes were put to work on the governor's land near Jamestown, and others were sent to outside settlements. At first the blacks worked as indentured servants, just

as whites did, and after about seven years were free to make a living for themselves. It was not long, however, before blacks faced a lifetime of servitude, and forty years later slavery became lawful in Virginia. Many more blacks were captured from Africa and traded as slaves in America in the following years because landowners found slavery a profitable form of labor. By the end of the seventeenth century, most of the colony's workers were enslaved Negroes.

At the same time that these newcomers to Virginia were denied their freedom, the Virginia Company gave to other Virginians "all liberties" of Englishmen everywhere, and ordered that they be governed by an assembly in addition to the governor.

The new democratic plan for the colony was more liberal than the English form of government. Virginians elected their own assemblymen and were to pay no taxes since the governor and other officials were to be supported from thousands of acres of public lands. Many tenants worked on these lands, and the profits from farming were to pay the costs of operating the colony. Six thousand acres were set aside near Jamestown for the governor, his council, and other officers, and much more land up and down the James River for other parts of the colony. Ministers were given free houses and small tracts of land, and ten thousand acres were set aside for a college. Every colonist who came was to receive fifty acres—and those who had bought stock in the company got one hundred acres.

In 1619 the new General Assembly of Virginia met for the first time. The assembly consisted of two parts: a small upper house called the Governor's Council, its members chosen by the Virginia Company, and a larger lower house called the Burgesses, elected by the freemen of the colony. On July 30, 1619, the governor, six councillors, and twenty-two burgesses sat in the new wooden church at Jamestown. The assembly had begun its life, the first of its kind in an English colony, and the oldest representative body in America.

The new lawmakers were full of ideas and passed many laws: No man should disturb the Indians and set off more wars, Indian children were to be educated, no man was allowed to loaf away his time, gamble, swear, get drunk, or spend too much money on clothes. In hope of starting a silk industry, the assembly ordered every settler to plant at least forty-two mulberry trees on his land in the first seven years. Tobacco prices were fixed, and poor leaf was to be burned. One law required that all colonists attend church twice on Sundays and that the men carry their muskets, ammunition, and swords.

The assembly not only made laws but sat as a court. In one case of this first session the court gave a painful sentence to Thomas Garnett, a lazy and troublesome servant accused of plotting to murder his master. Thomas was sentenced to have his ears nailed to a wooden pillory and to stand at the public post of punishment for four days—and to be whipped each day. Such was the work of the first elected governing body in America. The session lasted only six days and ended because the weather grew terribly hot and several members became ill. The Virginia Assembly continues to this day, with a history of very few, and very brief, inactive periods.

With the change of government and the coming of many new people, Jamestown was thriving, but the Virginia Company was losing money. The company found it very expensive to maintain a fleet and ship supplies to Virginia, and its leaders in England were becoming discouraged. An Indian attack in 1622 brought the company near ruin—and almost destroyed the colony.

Chief Powhatan had died four years earlier, and the new ruler of the tribes of eastern Virginia was Opechancanough (Opie-can-canoe), a wily leader who pretended to be friendly while he plotted to wipe out the entire colony. Only the year before, the chief had made a new treaty with the whites, and marked it by fixing a brass plate to a huge oak tree. Opechancanough said he would never break the peace—the sky would fall before he made war. Despite this pledge, the new chief had secretly organized the fighting men of his thirty-two scattered tribes, gathering them from their villages to lie in wait near the English settlements.

During the night of March 21, 1622, an Indian warrior slipped into the clearing of a house on the south bank of the James River, the home of a settler named Pace. The visitor went silently to a shed where his young brother slept, a boy called Chanco, who was a servant to Mr. Pace.

"We're going to attack all the whites in the morning," the warrior said. "You must kill Pace."

"But he is my friend," Chanco said.

"Kill him! He is an enemy like all other whites. We will drive them from our land. All of us will strike at once, on every farm, at every white man's fort."

Chanco was worried, for he had been treated kindly by Mr. Pace and had become a Christian. When his brother had gone, the boy went to his master and told him that the Indian tribes of Virginia planned to attack. Pace woke up his family and drove his farm animals into the house and barns, had many buckets of water drawn, and barred the doors. He had made the farm into a small fort, and his sons stood guard with their guns. While this was done, long before dawn, Pace rowed the three miles across the James and warned the people of Jamestown. They too put every man on guard and prepared to fight off an attack. As the sky in the east grew light, the colony waited, and every sentry kept watch on the dark woodlands.

When the Indians emerged during the morning, the settlers fired and soon drove them off. The town had been saved by the loyalty of the boy Chanco. Those who lived on the eighty other settlements and farms along the banks of the James were not so fortunate, for the long years of peace had made the Englishmen careless. They had come to trust their Indian neighbors, and the attacks came as a surprise.

And so on the quiet day of March 22, 1622, the settlers outside Jamestown went about their business as usual. Beyond the fort itself, there was not a whisper of attack. The chief and his men kept their secret so well that only Chanco took word of the raid to the whites. At exactly the same hour on this morning, Good Friday, the Indians struck.

Indians came to the houses of the whites for breakfast, as they often did, and some had even been overnight guests. Others entered English houses as usual, bringing deer, turkeys, fish, and skins to trade. They sat down to eat with the white families—but suddenly jumped up and killed their hosts with knives, axes, or tools, striking old men and women and children as well. Indians ran into the fields and killed Englishmen who were planting corn and tobacco. They went through the villages killing others who were making bricks, sawing, or building houses. The Indians burned houses, destroyed crops, and killed cattle. They cut up many bodies and carried the heads into the woods, shouting in triumph.

More than three hundred and fifty colonists were killed during that morning, many of them within a few miles of Jamestown. Six councillors were murdered, among them John Rolfe, at his plantation on the bank of the river. Twenty women were taken as captives to Indian villages, where they were kept for more than a year. The terrified settlers deserted many plantations and crowded into Jamestown and other fortified settlements, where they lived for many weeks.

The new governor, Sir Francis Wyatt, acted quickly to save the colony. He sent soldiers to command at every plantation, with orders to keep watch by night, to permit no one to talk with an Indian, and to have settlers move about in groups, carrying arms wherever they went. Once more the colonists attacked and burned Indian villages, killing many people. The governor also sent boats far up the Chesapeake to buy or seize corn from other Indian tribes.

The next spring Chief Opechancanough asked for peace, saying that enough blood had been shed. He offered to free the captive English women if the whites would allow his people to return to their villages on the York River. The council at Jamestown agreed, but only in order that the whites could take revenge. Spies went to the Indian villages, noted where corn was planted and when it would ripen, and then attacked without warning, murdering several chiefs and ruining Indian crops. One white expedition returned with several Indian scalps.

In the midst of this Indian war a dread disease known as the Plague was brought from England by sick passengers. The Plague spread rapidly through the colony, taking twice as many lives as had the Indian attacks. The men of Jamestown were hardly able to bury the dead. At one time in 1623 only one hundred and eighty whites were left to march against the tribes, and one hundred of these were unable to carry loads of supplies and arms. Yet, though Opechancanough had one thousand warriors who were skilled bowmen, the whites had guns which enabled them to win the war.

More hard times lay ahead. The colony was becoming overcrowded. Rich landowners held much of the good land in eastern Virginia, and more colonists were arriving each year. Soon there was not enough food, shelter, or good water for all the settlers. One Spanish spy reported that half of the people of Jamestown died each year. The effort to grow silk worms failed, Virginia grapes made poor wines, and crops dried up in the heat. A new glassworks at Jamestown burned twice and was then destroyed by angry Italian workmen who had become frustrated by inferior working conditions and few supplies. After many such reports from Virginia, King James ended the lottery which had helped to support the colony. When he saw that the Virginia Company could no longer pay the cost of the settlements, he placed Virginia under control of the crown, making it the first royal colony in British history. For the next fifteen years Virginia governed itself almost as before. The governor was responsible to the king instead of to the Virginia Company, but the assembly was still elected by the people. Together they continued to make and enforce local laws.

By now the colony seemed safe and secure. Other English colonies had been founded in New England (first called North Virginia). The earliest of these was on Massachusetts Bay in 1620, and others grew in Connecticut and Rhode Island and New Hampshire. A few years later a part of Virginia was set aside for the Maryland colony at the head of Chesapeake Bay, and other Englishmen settled to the south, in Carolina and Georgia. Jealous Virginians defied the king and resisted the coming of the Maryland settlers, and for a time there was fighting and bloodshed between

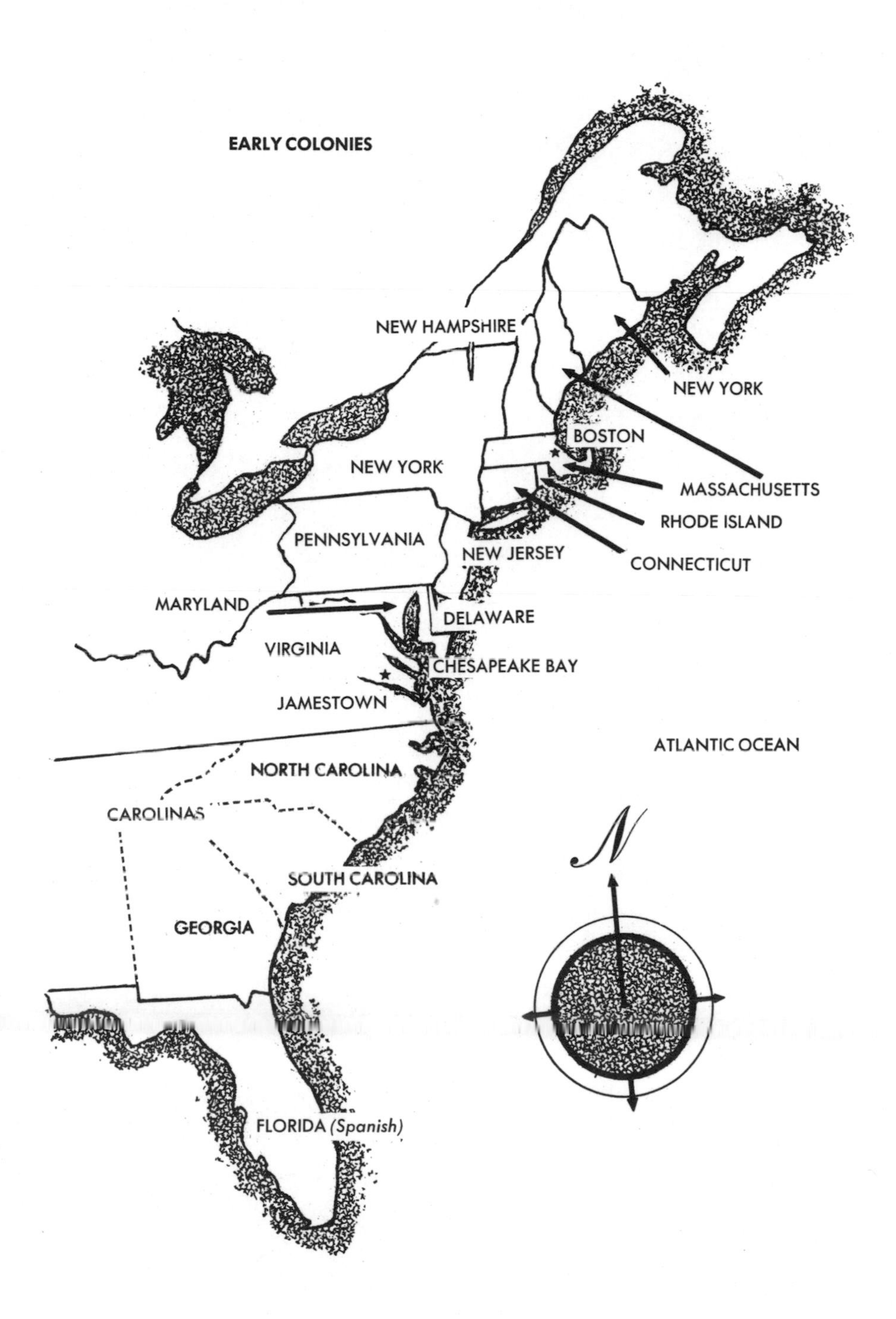
EARLY COLONIES
NEW HAMPSHIRE
NEW YORK
BOSTON
NEW YORK
MASSACHUSETTS
RHODE ISLAND
CONNECTICUT
PENNSYLVANIA
NEW JERSEY
MARYLAND
DELAWARE
VIRGINIA
CHESAPEAKE BAY
JAMESTOWN
ATLANTIC OCEAN
NORTH CAROLINA
CAROLINAS
SOUTH CAROLINA
GEORGIA
N
FLORIDA (Spanish)

the two settlements. The struggle soon ended, and the king's plan was a success: British colonies now stood side by side along most of the Atlantic Coast.

Within Virginia, adventurous settlers moved farther from Jamestown. In 1633 the colonists built a log palisade across the narrowest part of the peninsula between the York River and the James River—a log wall four miles long, so high that it could keep out Indians and prevent livestock from running away. Plantations were cleared on the York River, one of them on the spot where the city of Yorktown was to rise. The owner of this plantation was a refugee from France, Captain Nicholas Martiau, an ancestor of both George Washington and Queen Elizabeth II of England.

Already, lands near Jamestown were beginning to wear out from the raising of tobacco crops every year, and planters began to seek new land. They moved westward along the rivers James, York, Rappahannock, and Potomac, and the Virginia frontier was pushed rapidly forward. Yet the capital at the village of Jamestown remained the heart of the colony. There the General Assembly, passing more laws and taking more authority at each session, made a pattern of government that was to influence America for centuries. When the assembly sat each year, hundreds of people crowded the village to try cases in court, to hear the passage of new laws, to secure more lands, or to seek protection from Indians. At these "public times" the crowds also drank ale, played cards, watched entertainers, and talked over news of the day.

By this time the first wooden huts had disappeared, and brick houses rose in Jamestown, many of them huddled together in rows, like those in London and other English cities. Roads began to wind through Virginia, connecting Jamestown with other settlements. Counties were formed and local governments grew, each of them largely independent, with officers appointed from Jamestown. By 1630 there were more than twenty-five hundred people in Virginia, most of them near Jamestown—and five years later the population had doubled. Most of the newcomers were indentured servants brought over because their masters were given fifty acres of land for each servant. These men seldom settled in Jamestown but went instead into "the forest," the great land outside the capital.

Virginians had now become so independent that they dared to defy King Charles I, who had come to the British throne in 1625. The king was disappointed in the poor tobacco crops and a low return on his investment in Virginia, and he demanded that the Jamestown assembly agree to a contract regulating the price and quality of tobacco under full control of the crown. The assembly refused to approve this monopoly, and the king and Jamestown planters continued to quarrel at long distance for years, while tobacco prices remained low and money in Virginia scarce.

The men of Jamestown also moved boldly in other ways. A new governor, Sir John Harvey, who was stern and short-tempered, made enemies among his councillors, who met secretly and plotted to remove him from office. In the spring of 1635 this struggle between Jamestown's leaders broke out in a mutiny. When Governor Harvey ordered a carpenter, the servant of a planter, to build a small boat for government use without his master's consent, angry councillors scolded the governor for breaking the law and robbing planters of their rights. Public meetings were called and charges against the governor were read by prominent leaders, including the sheriff and Captain Martiau of Yorktown.

Governor Harvey arrested these men and charged them with mutiny and treason. The councillors grew so angry that they almost had a fist fight with the governor. At last their leader, Captain Samuel Mathews, told Harvey grimly, "Sir, the people's fury is up against you and it is beyond our power to appease it, unless you please go to England, and there to answer their complaints."

"The King appointed me to this office," Harvey said, "and I will not leave until he sees fit to recall me."

The councillors called in armed troops, for the governor had recently knocked out the teeth of one member with a club. After a bitter quarrel of several days, Harvey agreed to leave the colony and sailed for England to continue the squabble there. He won his case in London, returned to Virginia, and had his enemies imprisoned for a time. The long struggle was one more disturbing sign to English officials in London—these men who had gone to Virginia were becoming fiercely independent, so that no power could control them; Virginians would dare anything where their rights were at stake. These were men of a kind unknown in Europe, many of them leading several different lives, as merchant, land trader, Indian fighter, public official, and country gentleman. They were growing wealthy in the New World, living in good houses, and ordering what they needed from England, yet they were facing a wild frontier and meeting daily hardships undreamed of in London.

GOVERNOR WILLIAM BERKELEY

The rebel leader, Captain Samuel Mathews, lived on a rich plantation near Jamestown, with a view of the broad river. A writer of his day described the place: "He has a fine house . . . he sows yearly crops of hemp and flax, and has it spun; he keeps weavers and has a tan-house where leather is dressed, has eight shoemakers at work, has forty Negro servants and trains them to trades in his house. He yearly sows much wheat, barley, etc. The wheat he sells at four shillings a bushel; kills many cattle and sells them to ships when they come there, has plenty of livestock, a fine dairy, pigs and poultry. . . . In a word he keeps a good house, lives bravely, and is a true lover of Virginia, he is worthy of much honor."

A strong new governor was needed to deal with such men, and in 1642 Governor William Berkeley was sent from London. He was young and wealthy, well educated, had friends and relatives of influence in England, and had seen much of the world. Berkeley did not trust the common people with a part in government and once wrote, "I thank God we have no free schools nor printing and I hope we shall not have [for] these hundred years." The governor became friendly with the proud Virginia settlers who had made fortunes in the new land, and for several years he brought peace to the colony. Quarrels were few, new treaties were signed with the Indians, and Virginia and Maryland agreed on their boundaries in the Chesapeake. A poll tax, which had been paid to the governor, was repealed, and taxes on the poorer people were reduced. After the first assembly, the burgesses were so pleased with Governor Berkeley that they voted him a house and two orchards. Berkeley was to serve longer than any governor in Virginia's first century and to have great influence on American history.

Governor Berkeley was firm in religious matters and enforced the law which made the Church of England the only official church in Virginia. When Puritan ministers came from New England in the 1640's, Berkeley had them driven out. Other Protestant churches were unwelcome.

About this time Virginia was struck by a second terrible Indian massacre. In more than twenty years since the first attack, settlers had grown weary of wars with the natives and trade had been revived. Whites and Indians had become friendly once more, and the settlers had again grown careless.

The chief, Opechancanough, had never forgotten his hatred of the whites, though he was now so old that he had to be carried about on a litter and had servants to hold up his wrinkled eyelids when he wished to see something. The chief had been told of the civil war then raging in England, and decided that now or never he must "root out all the English," while they could get no help from their home country. He struck as he had before, without warning, against many white settlements at once. On April 18, 1644, warriors fell upon the frontier and killed more than five hundred whites. The attacks did not reach all settlements—Jamestown was again spared—and Governor Berkeley quickly marched against the Indian villages, killing and burning. Chief Opechancanough was captured and taken to Jamestown, where he was to be held until he could be sent to England. A soldier, in revenge, shot the old chief in the back while he was in prison.

This was the last of Indian wars in Virginia for thirty years. The new chief, Necotowance, made a treaty, saying that he held his territory by the grace of the King of England, to whom he would pay a tribute of twenty beaver skins each year when the geese flew north from Virginia. Indians were given the lands north of the York River and west of the falls of the James, and the whites were to hold the peninsula on which Jamestown lay, between the York and the James. Neither white nor Indian was to invade the other's territory, and all trading was to be done at frontier forts. When Indians went farther toward Jamestown, they were to wear striped coats to identify them as messengers.

From the new forts, far inland on the rivers James, Appomattox, and Chickahominy, traders began a new commerce with Indians of the unexplored interior. Pack trains carried goods deep into the wilderness, to return with loads of valuable furs for the London market. These pack trains were often long, with one hundred horses, each carrying a two-hundred-pound pack of guns, tomahawks, blankets, kettles, and trinkets. Whites continued to push westward despite the treaty, and the men of the frontier could not be controlled by officials at Jamestown. These traders gave the Indians of the American South and Southwest their first real contact with the world of the white man and took the first steps toward conquest of the interior.

By now Jamestown was forty years old, and the first children born in the colony were grown men and women nearing middle age. (In those days the average life was shorter than it is today.) Some of these men became Virginia leaders under Berkeley and formed a colonial court at his fine house, Greenspring, just outside Jamestown. This first generation of native Virginians served on Berkeley's council, on church vestries, county courts, and in the House of Burgesses, gaining experience in government. They were joined by a group of bold, vigorous young Englishmen called cavaliers, men who fled England when King Charles I was beheaded in 1649 and Oliver Cromwell became ruler of Great Britain. The newcomers began families which were to become prominent in Virginia life for many years to come, among them the Lees, Carters, Randolphs, Digges, Masons, and Pages. Many of these men had been army officers in England's civil war, and with them came a few titled cavaliers, two of whom, Sir Thomas Lunsford and Sir Henry Chicheley, became generals of Virginia militia and members of the council. Many other new people came to Virginia because of the troubles in England—merchants, farmers, skilled craftsmen, servants, and workmen. Together they changed the colony, giving it the leadership in business and politics which greatly influenced young America.

At Greenspring Governor Berkeley and his friends led a gay life, racing English horses, fox hunting, and holding balls and receptions. The "starving time" and Indian massacres seemed long ago. Berkeley was removed from office by Cromwell and retired to Greenspring, where he lived and entertained as usual, waiting for the monarchy to return in England so that he could become governor once more. Greenspring was the first mansion in the North American wilderness, a large, handsome brick house with a walled courtyard and many outbuildings. Berkeley's wife said it was "the finest seat in America and the only tolerable place for a Governor."

During these years, when there was less control from England, the assembly in Jamestown took over new rights, introducing its own laws and governing the colony almost as it pleased. Virginians never gave up these rights in later years. Even when Cromwell sent men to force Virginia to obey his commands, the colony won a compromise and was left free to tax itself and make most of its own laws—although it was against the law to speak well of the king or to read the Book of Common Prayer.

Jamestown went through another change in 1660, when King Charles II came to the English throne after Cromwell's death—and William Berkeley again became governor of the colony. In this term Berkeley was not so popular as before. He had become stern and short-tempered as he grew older, and the new king placed heavy burdens on Virginia. Dutch warships attacked English ships along the Virginia coast, crops failed once more, and the colony began to fill with convicts, beggars, gypsies, and the poor from England. Many children were kidnapped in London and carried to Virginia. Other troubles continued. The king levied new taxes and ordered the colonists to trade only with England, and not with foreign shippers, a law which made English merchants rich and Virginia planters poor. Virginians began to murmur complaints against Governor Berkeley, though he was not to blame for most of these problems.

By now Berkeley had more power than had previous governors of Virginia and did almost as he pleased. As he aged, the governor became more stubborn and irritable. Only three councillors were left, and Berkeley forced them to do as he wished. He kept the same House of Burgesses in office for fourteen years, refusing to

call a new election, because these men were friendly to him. He called courts to sit when he pleased, rather than on dates set by the assembly. In counties outside Jamestown, officials met secretly to pass high taxes—and to exempt themselves and their friends. Poor men were forced to pay more taxes than their rich neighbors who owned thousands of acres. People began to hold meetings of protest and to grumble openly against the government.

At this time a new Indian war broke out in Virginia, and many settlers were killed. Berkeley built frontier forts and sent armed patrols through the country, but raids continued. Men said that the governor refused to attack the Indians because he wanted to continue to trade for beaver skins. When the leading planter, William Byrd, reported that Indians had killed three of his men, Berkeley said Byrd had made up that story as an excuse to start an Indian war. In 1676 planters on the south bank of the James rose in defiance of Berkeley, asking that someone lead them against the Indians despite the governor's orders. The leader who went to them was Nathaniel Bacon, Jr., a young councillor still in his twenties, handsome and bold and a powerful public speaker. He had just come from England, where he had been well educated and trained in the law. He was related to Governor Berkeley by marriage.

NATHANIEL BACON, JR.

Bacon led the planters against the Indian villages, and Berkeley took an army to the frontier in pursuit. He could not catch Bacon or his men, who marched to the Carolina border and wiped out an Indian tribe by attacking and burning its fort. Berkeley declared Bacon a traitor and removed him from the council, but the people supported their young leader, and volunteers guarded his house day and night to protect him.

Bacon was captured when he made a secret midnight visit to Jamestown, and was brought before the House of Burgesses under arrest. As Bacon entered the room, Governor Berkeley said, "Now I behold the greatest rebel that ever was in Virginia." He asked Bacon if he admitted his guilt, and when the rebel had done so, the governor pardoned him. "God forgive you," Berkeley said. "I forgive you."

Bacon returned to his seat on the council and was promised a commission to fight against the Indians—but only because the governor feared that the armed people would overthrow the government to support Bacon.

When Bacon returned to his farm without a commission, his angry neighbors marched with him to Jamestown, about six hundred strong, and, with his armed guard around the statehouse, demanded a commission. The seventy-year-old governor refused, shouting that Bacon was a rebel and a traitor. He then bared his breast and cried, "Here! Shoot me! I'm a fair mark, shoot!" He drew his sword and dared Bacon to fight, but the young man turned away.

Bacon ordered his men to cock their guns and aim at the burgesses, who finally begged the governor until he signed a commission for Bacon. Bacon's followers demanded new laws, taking away some of Berkeley's powers. These laws were passed the next day. Elections were to be held more frequently, and the method of passing taxes were changed. But the people were not content. Bacon tried to take over the government of Virginia and led his army to besiege Jamestown. He fired on it with cannon, drove the governor to flight, and burned the capital city to the ground, including the church and the statehouse. But just as he had won victory and had Virginia in his power, Bacon died of an illness, probably from exposure in the cold, muddy trenches at Jamestown. Many of his followers were executed by Berkeley, and as the last members of Bacon's band were hunted down, the rebellion came to an end, a part of the long fight for liberty in Virginia. Soon afterward, Governor Berkeley returned to England, where he died.

The burned village of Jamestown was rebuilt, larger than before, and continued for more than twenty years as the center of Virginia life. New governors came to struggle with the leaders of the colony, which grew westward toward the mountains. But in 1698, when an accidental fire destroyed Jamestown's fourth statehouse, the assembly voted to move the capital to higher ground, some six miles away. This spot in the forest, known as Middle Plantation, soon became Williamsburg, one of America's first cities built by a town plan. A new college, William and Mary, the second in America, was already rising there.

The charred bricks of the burned statehouse were dug from the wreckage and hauled to Williamsburg, to be used in the new Capitol building. Jamestown's day was over, after ninety-two troubled years as the cradle of British America. Today the dead of Jamestown's early years lie in their graves, and the ruins of the place are still there on the marshy bank of the river, a few exposed brick foundations and the remains of an old brick church. A tall statue of Pocahontas looks out over the land where the Indian princess played as a child, where she was baptized, married, and carried off on her last journey. The broad James River still surges past to the sea. Otherwise, there is little to mark the spot where modern America was born.

Important Dates in Jamestown's History

April 26, 1607—Three English ships, with 144 settlers aboard, anchor in Chesapeake Bay.

May 13, 1607—The colonists land at Jamestown.

May 26, 1607—Indians attack Jamestown fort and are driven off.

Winter, 1607–1608—John Smith is captured by Powhatan's tribe and saved by the chief's daughter, Pocahontas.

January 2, 1608—Captain Christopher Newport arrives with first reinforcements for colony and finds only 38 survivors in Jamestown.

September 10, 1608 to July, 1609—John Smith is president of the colony.

October, 1608—Second group of reinforcements arrives with two women; one of them, Ann Burras, is married in the first English wedding in the colony.

Spring, 1609—The Virginia Company issues a new charter under which London companies and businessmen hold stock in the colony.

August, 1609—Lord De La Warr, the first governor, arrives with 300 men, women, and children.

Autumn, 1609—John Smith returns to England.

Winter, 1609–10—Four hundred and thirty Jamestown settlers die in the "starving time."

June 7, 1610—Survivors leave for England but return to the settlement when they meet Lord De La Warr.

May, 1611—Sir Thomas Dale arrives with 300 reinforcements and supplies and becomes governor.

1611 or 1612—John Rolfe plants seed from sweet West Indies tobacco and founds a new Virginia industry.

April 5, 1614—Rolfe marries Pocahontas.

1619—Virginia Company establishes liberal and more democratic form of government in Virginia. Eleven ships arrive with more than 1,200 people, including 90 young women to marry colonists.

July 30, 1619—The General Assembly of Virginia, the first representative body in America, meets for first time.

August, 1619—Twenty African Negroes reach Jamestown in a Dutch ship and are traded in exchange for food. The blacks work as bonded servants.

March 22, 1622—More than 350 colonists die in Indian massacre.

1633—Log palisade built between York and James rivers. The banks of York River are settled.

1635—Colony's leaders rebel against Governor Sir John Harvey.

April 18, 1644—A second great Indian massacre kills more than 500 whites. Governor William Berkeley invades Indian territory, destroying villages. Chief Opechancanough is captured and killed.

1676—Bacon's Rebellion breaks out against Governor Berkeley, and small armies fight for control of colony. Bacon dies October 26.

1698—Fire destroys the fourth capitol building at Jamestown, and the Assembly plans to rebuild in Williamsburg.

Index

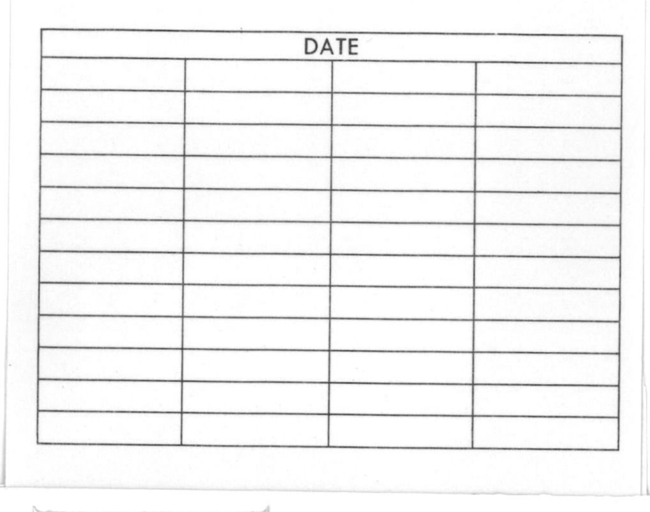
DATE

507003 B
00640

DISCARD
TRINITY LUTHERAN SCHOOL
MORRISTOWN, MINN. 55052